T0381296

A TRIP OF A LIFETIME

July 5th–July 31st, 2008

LORETTA KIER

AuthorHouse™
1663 Liberty Drive
Bloomington, IN 47403
www.authorhouse.com
Phone: 1 (800) 839-8640

Published by AuthorHouse 11/30/2018

ISBN: 978-1-5462-6569-6 (sc)
ISBN: 978-1-5462-6570-2 (e)

Library of Congress Control Number: 2018912793

Print information available on the last page.

Any people depicted in stock imagery provided by Getty Images are models,
and such images are being used for illustrative purposes only.
Certain stock imagery © Getty Images.

This book is printed on acid-free paper.

TRIP OF A LIFETIME

JULY 5TH - JULY 31ST, 2008

TABLE OF CONTENTS

Front of our R.V.

DEDICATION

This book is dedicated to Charlene H. Kirkner and in the memory of her life. She was a person who gave so much to so many. She took care of the little people in this world. She knew the true meaning of suffering and the courage of love. She also gave her time in taking care of them. Her love for their causes did have a price tag and she paid it every time. As my very best friend, she understood me. Yes, she had to let go of this world and leave, but she will live in my heart forever. She always lit up a room with her smile and always had a kind word to say. When I was down, she picked me up. You could ask for nothing more in this life, but having her as your best friend. Her beautiful light snuffed out, her lovely flame died and the smoke got in my eyes. To this day, I cry. In the big picture of life, Char has encouraged me to run the race. To live life honestly, to never forget to play and to love as if there is no tomorrow. And in the end remind me each day that miracles do happen, and has shown me that my heart can hold more love and joy than I ever dreamed possible. She was the sweetest person everybody knows. You don't know what to call her, but she was mighty like a rose. August 19th 1946 to May 2nd, 2009,

The second dedication in my book is to my son James Joseph Kier Jr. who died suddenly on Wednesday, May 9, 2018. He was born on August 1, 1975 in Norristown. He was my fifth children and fourth son.

The only thing Jim loved more than the Super Bowl champion Philadelphia Eagles was his family. Family was special to him. Adored his wife Katie and his four daughters Savannah -16 years old, Addison- 3 years old, Eleanor- 2 years old and Grace-8 weeks old. His siblings Thomas Kier and his wife Larisa, Robert Kier and his wife Ramona, Joseph Kier and his wife Michelle, Jennifer Kier and her wife, Melody. Also his many nieces and nephews. He was the fun and laughter of all family gatherings. Jim loved being surrounded by friends and family and his dogs. He loved his dogs and really all dogs.

He loved his job as a crane operator and he is a loyal member of Operating Engineers, local 542. Jim had many hobbies including dirt bike, building and racing cars, hunting shooting and of course pyrotechnic displays on the fourth of July. Since I was born on the fourth of July, he always enjoyed my birthday.

As a single mom, my children were always number one in my life. He touched my heart deeply because he lived just 10 minutes away always there he made Holidays. Sports game and just a cook out. He made my life worth living just by being around.

Jim I meant this little message: *Jim never feel that you are alone. No matter how near or far apart, I am always right there in your heart and you are in my heart. Just believe in yourself and remember you only fail when you stop trying. Someday, we will be together again, someday.*

Our God has told us we would be together again but until then, my heart has a big hole that hurts but never forget and I will do the same, no matter what the fact that I love you.

Sunrise

Aunt Char and Savannah

CHAPTER 1

Today is a wonderful day. School is out for the summer. The sun is shining, Char is mowing, and the flowers are growing. The river is flowing, and the boaters are rowing. The farmers are hoeing; Jimmy and I know that this is going to be the best summer of all. Tonight, we are having a meeting at Aunt Char's house with the twenty-five little people who live in Aunt Char's barn. One year ago, they moved from our barn in Glenmore to Aunt Char's barn in Skippack. There, they make miniature furniture for Char's shop, From the Past, the largest miniature furniture shop in the state. Tonight, we will start our planning for our trip in our RV across the United States. In our meeting tonight, there will be twenty-five little people who will be coming with us on our trip. There are still thirty-five little people who will stay behind with Aunt Char, keeping their business going, and Savannah will be helping Aunt Char. These are the little people who will be coming with us: the two leaders of the village, Hans and Victor; the two schoolteachers who will be taking pictures and writing a journal, keeping a history of the whole trip; five children who are ten or older and were chosen because of their high marks throughout the school year; two people who will do all the laundry and keep the little people's RV clean; two kitchen prep workers to help the chef; and most importantly, nine men from the little people's rescue squad. They can save any little person who falls in any little crack or gets hurt and has to be rescued. The remaining little people coming are the medical staff, some doctors and nurses. Han's wife and two children will also be in the group. My family and the group that will be riding in and taking care of our RV will be my mother; my grandmother, who will be doing most of the driving; Jimmy; and me. We also will be meeting up with my grandmother's friend Debbie Higginbotham in Oregon. She will be with us for ten days of our journey. Debbie, whose nickname is Bones, owns and directs the Willamette Ballet Academy in Woodburn, Oregon, and is on the board with my grandmother for the rock star and singer Storm Large, whose picture is going to span the whole back of our RV. Storm Large, whose picture spans the whole back of our RV. This picture advertises her new play in 2009 and now is brought back for its ten-year anniversary, on June 25, 2019 for eight shows in Portland, Oregon at Portland Center Stage. An autobiography, musical written and performed by Storm Large, "Crazy Enough" is about staying alive and living fully in the moment. Part cabaret, part confessional and part comedy, the show reveals how she grew up with a schizophrenic mother and the way music helped her to overcome heartache. In painful and humorous detail. Storm Large takes her audience on a gritty journey, showing us what it takes sometimes just to survive. Yes, an empowering look at how one woman has managed despite repeated heartaches and screw-ups to stay aware of the preciousness of life. Now, storm has written a book called, "Crazy Enough". Now, the days leading up to our departure will be very busy. For the next week, everyone will have a notepad to write down things that we really need. Packing the RV is a job that must be carefully done. There are many things and only so much room. There is also only so much weight that can go in the RV. I was told that along with everything else, the RV carries so much water. There is white water, which is fresh water that you use for cooking and washing, and then there is a section for the grey water, which is dirty water. We will have to stop along the way at dumping stations to drain out the old water, so that weight will always be changing. All of the other weight in the RV will remain the same, and that should be a very steady weight. Everywhere in our house, we have notes hanging up about what we are taking, like food and drinks. One great thing is that the water for the little people had become a lot easier to get. They once had to only gather rainwater, because the rain water had no salt in it. Now in the market, they sell salt-free water. Regular groundwater contained so much salt that for the little people that it would affect their kidneys, and they could die from it. So their golden rule was to only drink rainwater. Now we don't even have to gather that anymore. It is going to make our trip a lot easier, and of course, it is going to solve that big problem for the little people.

My journal tonight is done with the leader of the little people, Hans. I had asked Hans what he felt the little people's main focus was on, and he came up with giving! First, giving to each other makes them very strong to help others. Their time is the most priceless thing they have. It gives hope to others, which brings about love. Love is the strongest force in life. Because of love, people fulfill their dreams. Fulfillment in life keeps hope alive and makes our love stronger. It brings about a drive to make us stronger—a never-ending circle. This has also given them a far greater appreciation of the countless acts of giving they have witnessed all of their lives—and yes, taken for granted. And it has convinced us that almost everyone, even as small as we are, regardless of income, available time, age, or skill, can do something useful for others—and in the process, strengthen the fabric of our shared humanity. We the little people find a cause that we can help with. We get together and have a meeting, always looking at how much we can give. Then we talk to the whole village. Just lately, we helped a busload of children trapped in a bus crash. We helped with the whale that beached himself because he was depressed, thinking his wife and baby had been killed. It was good for him that we knew whale sound language. Hans had said without Jimmy, my mom, and me, we would not be able to give our help to anyone. This is another point: the giver needs help from others to be able to give. Everyone must find support to be able to give. Everyone must find people who want to make a difference. We find that the most rewarding act is to help people get a chance. That's often all one person can give another. But this is what makes all the difference. Hans was hoping that if I wrote this in my journal, and people read this, it would encourage others to give whatever they can, because everyone can give something. There's much to be done down the street and around this beautiful USA. It's never too late to start. We encounter givers right in front of our faces—old, young, and in between; rich, poor, and in between; highly educated, virtually illiterate, and in between. You'll read about innovative organizations, new ways of giving time and money, and old-fashioned acts of individual generosity and kindness. Hans thinks you'll find people with whom you can identify, groups you might want to join, companies you might want to buy from, and projects you might want to start on your own. It is impossible to mention all the individuals and organizations doing good work in America. There are millions of them. We hope the people and groups profiled are diverse and representative enough to persuade you that everyone can and should be a giver. I'm writing this to encourage you to join the ranks of givers.

Because my ending tonight would not be as perfect, I add the following:Rafting with Her Family

Written by Bones, the best addition to my journalWe headed out toward Maupin, a small desert town on the Deschutes River in central Oregon. We were excited to go, since it was before the summer's heat that would lower the water level's intensity and speed of the river. Oregon's snow caps were melting, and the river flow was abundant and wild. We arrived there and signed in, were given life jackets, and were instructed on how to use them. We were told to only wear what we would in the shower, and most likely, we would get very wet and shouldn't bring anything that would get damaged.

We were given an oar and told to climb into the raft. We sat halfway on the side of the raft. We were instructed to work as a team, and we practiced rowing in unison, going forward, backward, and turning left and right. We started down the river, working on our technique. The guides let us know where the birds and animals of the region were. We tried to get a glimpse of them on the shore. They told us about the native American Indians of the region, and we tried to look for their carved drawings in the small cover off the riverbanks. We learned how to go through the rapids by paddling quicker, not slower. We learned to drop down fast to the floor of the raft so the splash of the water would go over us when we went down the Devil's basin. It turned out to be a calm and cool ride, accentuated by the occasional whitewater rapids, which we were expertly guided through by our instructors. At times, the guides told us stories about other groups that had gone on the rides as well. One fan favorite was President Obama; he was there the week before with his family and bodyguards. It was not publicized and kept as a private family outing so the First Family could enjoy themselves.

They are usually told to put their car keys near the gas cap or on the driver's side front tire, but you see Sunday rafters with their rafts overturned. Out went their ice chest with their keys, cell phones, and wallets in the river. They were very frantic, for everything they needed to get home was in the river. Another important thing told to us was that if you fall out of the raft, do not walk on sharp river rocks. Go belly up; point your toes up, and just float. Halfway through the trip, we were guided to the shore and served hot dogs, all kinds of different salads, drinks, and ice cream—all you could eat!

We got back on the raft after this big lunch with our stomachs full of food and our bodies lethargic from the rest. We had to finish our six-hour trip with the most wild rapids of the ride. We wanted to relax and sightsee but were asked to use our speed, strength, and energy like never before. We repeated the strongest rapids for the fun of it. I was excited, tired, sore, and wet. I thought, *It's best if one is young, like my sons, when doing this.* I chipped my tooth from dropping to the raft's floor too fast and lost my shoes in the wild waters.

We sat for a while in the desert heat under a tree and then headed home. Listening to my sons' stories of the raft ride and how doing it as a family meant something to them made the aches and pains my body felt worthwhile.

Bones and Grammy on the glass sky walk 250 feet out over the Grand Canyon

Jen, Grammy Mel at Mount Rushmore

Jenny and Mel at the Grand Canyon

It was a beautiful sunny bright day. The yellow of this day filled us up from our toes to our hearts, and from our hearts to our heads. When we got to the Grand Canyon, the park service made up their minds that Grammy, getting on and off their tour bus, was in danger and they didn't think they wanted to take that chance, so they gave us a personal forest ranger guide to take us around in his van. Boy, did this make it easier to transport the little people too, what a gift! When we got to the Grand Canyon's glass sky walk I knew from the start I could not go on it. I thought I could, but I knew it was too much, 250 feet out into the Grand Canyon, and then Grammy piped up, "I'm gonna go." Jimmy, Bones and Grammy will go. So I liked looking over the Grand Canyon, right at the cliff's edge, that was fine. Grammy, Jimmy and Bones went right up there and they took some of the little people with them. They had to put special booties on their feet, and Grammy was able to take her scooter on to it. They were so brave and the funny thing was that Bones had a shirt on that said "Thelma" and Grammy had a shirt on that said "Louise." That stopped a lot of people in their tracks, because they remembered in a movie that Thelma and Louise had driven their car, right into the Grand Canyon in that story. On the glass skywalk you look down 7,000 feet into the Grand Canyon, also this is where Grammy, Jimmy and Bones met up with the Indian Chief and the Chief got a peek at the Little People. Later, in the Tepee, he will be introducing them to the Indian's little people. But first we would have to chow down on an Indian lunch. Boy did it smell good. Buffalo Burgers, Buffalo Meat, cheese, melted over onions and flat bread. Indian bread! We all loved this food. It came along with corn and beans. That was sold in a food court to all that came to see the Grand Canyon from the skywalk. There were other little shops around it, little gift shops, and little places where you could talk to the Indians. They would show you their leather work, they would show you the jewelry that they made, the rings, bracelets and necklaces. It was beautiful and gave us a better understanding of how creative these Indians were. And it was right there on this site. On our trip of a lifetime we were treated very special! The Chief's wife did a special dance with silver charms hooked on her skirt made with a number of every day of the year. It was a fertility skirt and as she danced this dance of joy the clanging of these silver charms hitting together was as beautiful sound as the drums and the horns were that played in the background to her dance. Also the grandson to the chief, who was a top competitor dancer, he danced for us too, his feet moving as if they were on fire. As the tunes were beating out on the drums and the horns, we were taken up by the festival of the Indians, by their struggle in their dance they played out their stories. And in their dance they play out their grief and in their dance they also play out their joy. We were taken up by the Indians even in their struggle to this day to survive. One thing about the skywalk, it was a dream. A dream of David Jin, founder of the skywalk, just like the eagle can fly over the Grand Canyon, his envision was to enable visitors to walk the path of the eagle. That's why they call this Eagle's Point. There was a big eagle spread out in the canyon that was formed by the wind and the dust and it really did look like an eagle from a distance. I don't know what it would be like to be right on top of it because it was too far away and too high up for any man to go to. You kind of become surrounded by the Grand Canyon by standing at the edge of the glass bridge. The bridge is a chance to share the wonder of the canyon that the Hualapal tribe has generously offered all the money that is made from the tourist at the skywalk and the shops around it and in the food court, all of this money goes to the tribe. They won back 89 acres from the government, it belonged to them anyway, but they went to court and some way this tribe has won it back which helps them survive. As I stood and looked over the canyon with my mother, Grammy, Bones, Jimmy and I took in this view our day was filled with the wonderment of it all. And after lunch the Chief lead us into the tepee. There we were sitting on animal fur with the Indian Little People and our Little People were sitting with them the Chief spoke to us and told us his unbelievable stories that not only took us into being able to view the Indian feelings but also guided us like it guided the Indians to a place of understanding and a place of knowledge that we would have never had if we hadn't gone to the Grand Canyon. So I will write this story to you tonight just what the Indian Chief told us. The chief stood before us with the light from the fire glowing in his eyes. When he opened his mouth and spoke a pin could have dropped in this tepee, it was silent. The only sound was the sound of the wind in the canyons sweeping around the outside of the tepee. The chief told of his grandson's anger because his schoolmate had done him an injustice. And the chief said this:

"Let me tell you a story about my grandson, I too have felt a great hate for those that have taken so much with no sorrow for what they do. But hate wears you down, do not try to hurt your enemies it is like taking poison and wishing your enemy would die. I have struggled with these feelings many times for many years. It is as there are two wolves inside of me, one is the good one and does not harm. He lives in harmony with all around him when it is right to do so and in the right way. But the other wolf is full of anger. The littlest things will set him off to a fit of temper, he fights with everyone. There are times for no reason he can not think because his anger, his hate is so great. It is hard to live with these two wolves inside of me for both of them try to dominate my spirit. At the time the boy looked intensely into the chief's eyes and asked- "Which one wins grandfather?" The chief solemnly replied, "The one I feed." Then there was the time that a boy Indian was traveling in the desert, he had not taken enough water for the amount of heat that was happening that day. He looked up towards the mountain and he could almost smell the moisture and water coming from it. He knew of a spring up there, so he went on his journey up the mountain and when he got to the spring the water was almost dried up, and it was slowly dipping from a pool in the high up rocks above his head. He holds up his cup and he gathers the water drop by drop and as he is lifting his cup to his lips a falcon comes shooting down from the sky and he knocks the cup right out of the boys hand. The Indian boy was mad. He was angry. This happened two more times. He was very thirsty. He was very angry now though and he gets the falcon and he kills it. The cup had fallen from his grasp, it had fallen into the valley below. He couldn't get it so he decides to climb up the mountain and he would drink from a spring that is way above his head. But when he gets there he finds that in this pool of water was a dead poisonous snake. The falcon, oh my God, the falcon was trying to save his life, and in his anger he had killed the falcon. The chief said when you act in anger what is done can not be undone! Our prime purpose in this life is to help others and if we can't help them, at least don't hurt them. So focus, think through your actions. Don't become so angry that this anger poisons your brain. Anger poisons your body. The falcon was trying to save the Indian boy. There are savors around us all the time! Are we walking too fast that we can't see what is happening in front of us? What is happening behind us? What the consequences will bring to us? Do we get so angry we can not think? The brain. The brain controls our spirit. The spirit lives within. Our spirit sometimes has a vision of reality, but sometimes the reality is colored and it is bias. We are limited unless we use more of what our spirit has given us. We are limited if we do not keep our body and our spirit in peace with good, compassion with good focus. What I am telling you today is do not make the spirit sick, do not fill it with jealously, anger, hatred, revenge, and fighting all the time. Yes, fight when you have to, but fight the war in a just way. Do not steal from your neighbor, do not take his possessions, do not take his wife, do not take his tepee, do not take his furs. Keep your spirit happy, keep it in peace with the world and keep it in peace with nature. This is what I am trying to tell you find a balance, find a balance that brings us all to the same spot. Brings us The "Little People" and I were talking around the campfire tonight about the course of the Indians in America what they had and what was taken away from them. We see that over the years thousands of Indians were denied the chance to live their to the fullest and thousands still die needlessly every year. Because we live in an interdependent world we cannot escape each other's problems. These Indians are vulnerable to the spread of disease, and the potentially cilamitas effects of climate change. The fact that one in four people who die each year will succumb to AIDS, Tubercalosis, malaria, diabetes or infections related to dirty water cast a pall over their lives and their children's future. These people live in their village where the economic growth stimulated has not been broadly shared. Half of them live on less then $2 a day. The poverty rate among Indian families has risen. Increased outsourcing of production and services has intensified insecurity. These Indians are jobless, ill, disabled, isolated and ignored. Desperate taking hope to be better of the loss of hope knowing their children with dreams that will die without a helping hand. The modern world, for all its blessing is unequal, unstable, and unsustainable. So I, and the "Little People" were hoping that this world could start sharing the responsibility and share the sense of genuine belonging, based on the essence of every successful person to give in our common humanity is more important than our interesting difference. We came to the understanding by the end of our campfire that all of us can make a difference and help move America away from the poverty, disease and conflict that today Indians are having. Solving these problems we will need help from different foundations that have no idea how bad things are for the Indian. They need a bigger voice in Washington. It is a cause but help from the general public is what we need to make our efforts work. "Welcome every morning with a smile. Look on the new day on another special gift from your creator, another golden opportunity to complete what you were unable to finish yesterday. Be a self starter. Let your first hour set the theme of success and positive action that is certain to echo through your entire day. Today will never happen again. Don't waste it with a false start or no start at all. You were not born to fail." (Og Mandino) In watching the "Little People" go about their daily living or their trip and back have this theme is driven in there very being and they pass it on to their children. "Some days you will be the light for others, and some days you will need some light from them. As long as there is light, there is hope, and there is hope, and there is a way." (Jennifer Gayle)

Now in staying with our trip we know that the struggles in life must be fought with the family before you can help others you have to make the family stronger. The idea the "Little People" came up with is give the Indians land that we took, give them the training they would need and jobs to build their and the supplies needed to grow their own food, raise their own cattle. Don't just give them things, give them the chance to have the job on their own-giving them their life back. A long journal tonight with lots of thought and insight. Time for bed!

Bones and Grammy at Yellowstone National Park

Things we saw on the way to Yellowstone National Park

Bear dragging a deer killed on the road

A buffalo out on the road walking

Jen, Mel, Bones and Grammy eating at Old Faithful Inn dining room in Yellowstone National Park, WY

Now I wanted to share with you a story my Grandmother shared with me to know that anyone can be bullied. A sad thing happened on a school bus in Greece, New York, a bus monitor Karen Klein became an overnight celebrity in June when a group of vulgarity spewing middle schoolers targeted her for ridicule. They took a video of the whole bully event and put it on facebook-hitting her and calling her all kinds of names as she sat on the bus. A viral video of Klein's mistreatment triggered an outpouring of support, including $703,873 in donations from an online campaign begun by a Canadian matritionist. Klein, 68, is using $100,000 of the money to start a bullying awareness foundation. She finds the stories people share with her are very overwhelming. Stories from other adults who were bullied by kids in their neighborhood, and still others whose event through bullying as children can't seem to forget it. Now retired, she aims to help other victims of bullies. Now for the best thing that can happen from this chapter is that every child that is bullying, their parents help to put a stop to this happening, and that these children tell the person that are bullying that they are sorry. The person that has been bullied forgives them. The family and the school must work hand and hand together or something worse is going to happen to all of these people. Go on Klein's website and find out how to stop bullying. For this to really stop, we need everyone's help.

Often during our trip, music fills the RV. Grammy's favorite singer is Storm Large (her picture is 9x15 feet across the back of the RV-see back cover.) Storm speaks out for all the outcast, underdogs and bullied. She was picked on in her younger years but has shown everyone that regardless of the people around them they can make it. She is a brilliant role model because what she was able to do with her life. She is known to make people feel stronger with her songs. She has a performance that truly moves you. It transfixes you and then alters your being. You either become different or see things differently Grammy is swept away by the beauty of her thoughts by the essence. The beauty is in her bravery, to show herself and to embrace struggle and win. She is genuine in everything she does be it song-story or plays she writes whether it's her vocal presentation or her persona. Storm shows the power of Freedom and passion. She gives herself complete freedom to be who we are and she is and to embrace life as a person worth something. She gives everyone permission to be strong in their struggles in life. Two songs that you should look up on you tube by Storm Large are "Fat Chicks Revenge" and "Stand Up for Me". These songs will make you stronger.

Homosexuals, the gay people, oh my gosh you see that as awful right away, if you see somebody is different right away they are picked on. In 33 of our states a person can be fired if they are gay. The other thing is that suicide is four times greater for people who are bullied for being gay. How can we interfere with love, how can we interfere with how somebody feels about someone else? That is none of our business. Bullying is the beginning of this problem. Yes and maybe today it is greater because of the internet, we have seen lately people dying and committing suicide because of things on the internet. It spread so fast, it spread so far! As a teen when they see things like bullying, they kind of let it happen, because they are not thinking of the consequences. All this teenager is thinking of is, that they want to fit in, they want to part of it, and if they were to step out of line and say something then this would put them in a difficult spot. Oh yes, I understand when the little people say they have never experienced it and because they have never experienced it, and they don't have this feeling engraved in their mind that they should be picking on someone. You are picked on for being black, for being white, for being Indian and gay, this is not okay unless people stick up and get in charge and start controlling this situation we are in trouble. Is it only the beautiful girls get to be cheerleaders? Are they the only ones who get to be the prom queens? We see this all the time, we single them out, we see them at school dances. The shy, the awkward, we see them on the sideline. We have to start setting new rules. We have to make rules that people follow. Is it the weak that only get bullied? It seems like it. Shouldn't parents be teaching their children to not let this happen? Isn't it the parents that should be putting their foot down? Do we not have time? Is making money the only thing on their mind? It is about time we do some new parenting. So if it was to start in the home, if the parent would take a strong hold on this problem, it wouldn't be the same. The schools do what they want to do, they make the rules but if a parent steps up and tells the school what the new rules should be, because this problem is getting out of hand. Then this would carry over into everyday life. The home parenting is failing very bad here, as a family we have to become stronger in teaching the child right from wrong, in this problem the bullying has to stop and it has to start at home. If the father and mother don't set the rules in place, when the child is very young, then bullying will never stop. When I was a little girl playing on the playground, my mother was there watching me, if we got into a fight she would take us a side and find out why. And if we were wrong we were put in to time out we knew that during the time that mom was there we had to play nice or we don't get to play. We never could make it fun for everyone if you were calling kids names. Or you got the consequences you were in time out! So the parents made the rules on the playground when we were playing at home the parents were there watching. Where are the parents? The parents should be making sure that bullying is handled at a very young age, then make sure at the school playgrounds, at the churches, on the busses. Standing at the bus stop, there should be someone there to govern it, to make sure that the rules are being followed. No bullying! Yes, it starts at home, family should take time to talk about this problem. It has gotten way out of hand. One week in September five children died. Why? Because of bullying! I am writing this to all that are reading my journals the thing I have learned and the trust that was taught was the right thing to do. I have learned it from my family first, from people that loved me the most. I trust the most and obeyed the rules so when I was told to be nice to my friends, to my classmates, or just people I see at the park I do that because that is what the people that love me have taught me. So the way it looks and in the eyes of the little people here sitting around the campfire if your child bullies anyone it is the mother and the fathers fought. When I grow up I will never let my child bully anyone! We need help from everybody. We need help from teachers at school, we need help from society. When our government starts speaking out say for gays, letting people get married no matter who they want to marry it is none of their business. Letting people be in the armed forces to fight for our countey without dropping them out or signaling them out because of who they love. Yes, fighting for our country without a problem. This is so strange that we would interfere and we would let even our senators and the congressmen not vote for love? Not vote for the freedom that everyone should have? The families and our government must start doing their job better. They must start doing the right thing! It all starts with the child. We must start to take care of our weak, not to pick on them, we must start by verbally teaching the new golden rule. "Love one another as you love yourself!" This is why the little people in the village stress no fighting, they have no way, they have no bullying, nobody taunts another person. These things are frowned upon. In society as a whole we must start frowning upon the wrong. The wrong that is done against people, because of their nationality, because of how they look because of what they feel, none of this should be held against the person. And I am hoping that as they renew their family ties as you start, they take vacation together, get into the campground of America. Rent a log cabin, get away from TV, get away from the computer, get away from the distractions of life and get down to the real meaning of why we are here. Find the right reason, moms and dads have to start preparing the child to walk the right way, take the right path follow that yellow brick road. The journey is hard but you know what? You never have to do it by yourself and if the parent doesn't start stepping in and the parent doesn't take control for their responsibility then things will never change. The family unit will never get stronger unless we stay together on this. Unless we make the rule golden again. Yes, I am telling young Jimmy when he grows up to be the best father that he can be. I am counting on me too. When I grow up I want to be the best mother I can be. We have had good role models. Everyone has to start being a good role model if they are a parent. Then all these young children will know how to act. They will show kindness, they will be loving to people they don't even know. We will not look at people for their weaknesses, but we will look at people for their strengths. Come on, is it really not that hard? No! Will it take a little time? Yes! If you feed your child food and nourish the body, you should feed your child thoughts that will nourish the mind! I am going to end tonight and the campfire burns, Grammy, mom, Bones, Jimmy, myself and all the little people on a wonderful note. Tomorrow is a new day, we can always start over. You be the guide to change the way our society looks at the weak. Be the good Samaritan. When you are walking through a park all dressed up on the way to work, carrying those briefcases, being blessed and having a job that you use your brain with. Look around and see. If your brain thinks and it should start at home! Yes, bullying, why do we have bullying in our world? I don't understand this. Does society tell us it is okay to bully? It seems that where ever I go, church, school, the mall, playing in the park. In these places, someone is being picked on! Do we promote this in our society? Maybe not up front, but in a way we are not stopping it, not interfering with it, not bringing up this rule to not pick on another person, this starts with each individual, starts with each family. So the training starts at home, but in our world it seems like someone is giving permission to do this, someone is saying, "Hey, it is okay to do this." But it is not! Our parents tell us don't lie, don't steal, don't curse but I never hear the teachers in school or the teachers in Sunday School say out loud you should not bully. This word is not used. Why is this? I can't understand enough to even explain it to the little people. Yes just lately my mother has said, when kids start bullying-walk away, don't be a part of it. In the news it seems like we had even points of distress with children that they have committed suicide. When death starts coming about because of a certain thing going on in society, we should step right in there. We should be the ones to change it. It has to start with the children. It seems like you can be bullied for about anything! Oh being too fat, being too skinny, being too short, being too tall, being too black, and being too white. Sure it is an easy thing to do, but isn't the bully the weakest person? What is wrong with these kids that they have to pick on another person? Knock a person down so they feel better, bigger and more worthy then the person they are picking on. At school where a child spends at least five or six hours a day why don't teachers jump in and stop bullying on the playground or in the halls? Stop the one who knocks the books out of a child's hand to make fun of him, to laugh at him. Boy they stopped stealing in school or you would get in a lot of trouble. They stop it when someone is hitting someone. You never see a teacher step in when someone is verbally picking on someone and verbally picking on someone is as bad as slapping them on the face. Even if this person is being picked on day in and day out there should be rules. There should be rules protecting them so that no one hurts them mentally. Because it is the day in and day out that wears the person down. Oh yeah I have heard some third grade teachers say, "Now that you are nine years old, now that you are a third grader you have to take care of this problem, you have to learn to take care of this yourself. This is not fair, because even the little people tell me that they are taught the weakest link in our chain is how strong we are-you must help the weak person to make him stronger and to be a strong society. Bulling should not exist.

Now this is going to be a special part in my journal. The subject has come up two or three times with the little people and now around our campfire tonight they brought it up again. Of course the Indian children have spoken about it and they get teased and taunted because they are Indian and mainly because they look like Indians. "Oh yeah, red skin." Is it only done by the white children? No! It is done by groups of children. Anyway it is called bullying. And in our society we have hit on it again. Mom and Grammy and both saw it happen to Jimmy. Of course Jimmy with a hearing problem and being the new kid on the block. He was teased a lot and taunted. Sometimes he misunderstands what some people are saying to him and you know that is the big problem-communication. The reason not to bully and not to pick on people should be a training that our parents work with us on, when we are very, very young. Now the little people have no bullying in their village, in their lives. They start at a very young age talking about unconditional love, talking about trusting each other and are very loyal and respectful to the parents. And even the parent's way of raising their children from very, very small that they don't bully, they don't tease and they don't verbally pick on each other. This is something we really have to look at and it is getting to be a problem in our society. And should we say that it starts at home? Yes! And the way to correct all to still have hope. A very fine man trying to give hope to all man was Dr. Martin Luther King Jr. who once said, "Darkness can not drive out darkness only light can do that. Hate can not drive out hate only love can do that. Hate multiplies hate! Violence multiplies toughness in a descending spiral of destruction. The chain reaction of evil must be broken or we shall be plunged into the dark ages of annihilation!" Help us to make the best decisions. Today we are bringing together two villages of very small people. They are not any less then we.

They have feelings like we do. It is the little person that seems to band together and in banding together their spirit becomes a big person. Listen to these little people. Encourage them, enrich them. They have so much to offer. They work together. One of the biggest things that I have learned from the little people is that they care and they love and they give equally and they do it by working together, by talking things out, by coming to a common ground and not fighting it out. Fighting it out poisons the spirits. You must learn to deal with life in a peaceful way. The chief went on to tell us his last story, his last truth. This story has been told in many fashions. It has been handed down from generation to generation. The white man tells of this story too. And I will tell you of the two travelers going through the desert, coming to the end of the mountain range they heard a voice. They stopped. They were afraid they were in enemy territory. They weren't at home and they were very, very frightened. But the light was shining and the voice was talking and it said get down from your horse. In their fear they did get down. They went over to the great light as it beckoned them there and it said to them, "See these stones on the ground? Put them in your pocket. And I will promise you tomorrow, you will be happy you did this and yet very sad." The men were scared. They were unarmed and they were not prepared for this. So they did as the voice at the light was saying. They picked up the pebbles and the stones on the ground. They filled their pockets. Then the voice said, "Get back on your horse and go! Take your horses from my land!" The men knowing that they were trespassing in a scared Indian area, they had no reasoning for this, but they were in fear from the stories of before. So they mounted their horses and they rode. They rode viciously and they would not stop. They rode all the way through the night. They were dead tired when they reached their home. Before they went to bed, they reached into their pockets, because the voice had said in the morning you will be happy but you will be very sad. They reached into their pockets and out they pulled gold, silver and diamonds. They had only taken a few because they were very frightened. They were happy they had taken some, but very sorry that they hadn't taken more if they would have known they could have filled their saddle bags if only they could have known. So what I tell you today is do not have regrets.

In ten springs from now in ten winters don't look back. Don't look back and say I wish I had. Do it all now. Live every moment to the richest. Face the sun everyday with a happy thought. Say good bye to the sun every day with a blessing. Don't let this time be wasted! Don't have regrets! Do it now, do it right, do all that you can! Do not drop out of school, do not run away from your destiny. Finish the job, finish it right. Take everything you can get out of everything that touches your soul. Keep your spirit happy! Yes, I am filled up tonight as I write in my journal. I am filled up. Jimmy, Grammy,

Bones, Mom the Little People and I sat around tonight before the day had ended, we watched that sun go down. What a beautiful sunset! We sat around the campfire, our second one that day. Our hearts were filled, our spirits were happy. Our soul knew, it knew that this had been a special day, not only for us, but for the Little People also. And maybe when you read my journal, you will feel good too.

A little P.S. here tonight in my journal, a little remark for Bones who had such good communications with the Indians, who they felt comfortable with. She set the day up so there were no weak spots, but everything we did had a purpose. It was such a productive day. And the Little People knew that we could count on Bones, when there is a schedule to be made, when there is a concert to get to, Bones is there! She puts her whole heart and her whole soul and her whole spirit into everything we did on this trip today, and maybe that's why we love her. Thank you Bones!

Bones (Deborah Higginbotham)

Bones and Fiona relaxing in the RV

Grammy's Notes on bullying:

At the 2017 Golden Globes speech by Meryl Streep: "the person asking to sit in the most respected seat in our country imitated a disabled reporter, someone he outranked, in privilege, power and the capacity to fight back" She said "It kind of broke my heart." So I'm also saying that I never thought we would have a president who has been a bully before. Meryl also went on to say "That when saw it and still can't' get it out of my head because it wasn't a movie, it was in real life. That instinct to humiliate when it's modeled by someone in a public platform, it filters down to everyone's life because it gives permission for others to do the same. Disrespect invites disrespect, violence incites violence. When the powerful use their position to bully others, we all lose." So please parents teach your children from the very start Bullying is bad. Loretta ???

What has happened to our World? What is the family looking at? In my experience we are fragile and in the election of 2016. People – the family ignored it. The mass incarceration of millions, the destruction of black communities, rampant poverty, addiction, illiteracy, no infrastructure to support a path forward. Life outside our bubbles has very precarious for decades. If we hadn't disenfranchised millions of black voters through incarceration for instance we probably wouldn't be in this mess. But our country is so fragile that we allowed a reality TV host, now puppet-president-elect to really take us down, are we now doomed? No but we should alarm every American. We need to check out. Have a prompt investigation of our election to support the senators checking thing out-calling for answers- we will be doomed if this is not done. They need support call your representative and senators and urge them to support these efforts. The family must become stronger, have a bigger voice. The children are the future. End

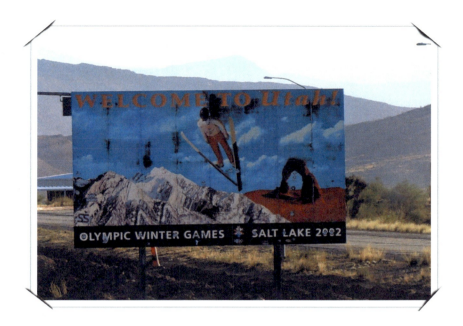

I DON'T CARE WHAT YOU
EARN, WHERE YOU LIVE,
WHAT YOU DRIVE,
WHETHER YOU ARE FAT
OR THIN, TALL OR SHORT,
BEAUTIFUL OR AVERAGE,
POOR OR RICH, SMART OR
NOT. IF YOU'RE MY FRIEND,
YOU'RE MY FRIEND.
I ACCEPT YOU FOR WHO
YOU ARE AND THAT'S ALL
THAT MATTERS …

**IF EVERYONE COULD
DO THIS BULLING WOULD
STOP. LOVE WOULD
GROW AND THIS WORLD
BE A BETTER PLACE.**

Grammy's Notes

Forgive yourself for not knowing what you didn't know before you learned it.

Buffaloes - Grand Teton National Park

Grand Teton National Park

Take your pet on your vacation.

We had Fiona our bull dog

Rocky Mts.

This story came from my grandmother who has so many regrets. It is full of the kinds of things that you pass over because until they happen you don't know what you have missed. That is why I am saying in this book that my plans are for you to pack your family up and go away together. Become part of these United States. See what other places look like. Take the freedom you have here in the USA and use it. Don't look back in 20 years and regret that you never traveled with your family, that they never had the chance to see the beautiful USA as a family. Hear the music of the times. Meet the people who wrote the songs. Music can bring all this to you.

Friday, August 15, 1969, was a hot, clear summer day. Even before the sun rose, long lines of cars—— new cars and old cars painted with slogans, sports cars, Volkswagons, pick up trucks, jeeps, trailers, almost anything on wheels——converged on route 17B, the road leading to Bethel, New York, where on Max Yasgur's dairy farm the stage was set for "three days of peace and music". Some 70,000 young people from all over the United States had paid $18 in advance to hear rock music at the Woodstock Music and Arts Festival. Perhaps twice that number was expected in the course of the weekend.

The earliest arrivals on Friday discovered that they were not the first comers. Far and wide, fields and pastures already were covered with tents. By seven o'clock in the morning every approach was clogged. The cars slowed, stopped and ground to a final halt. Now the only way to get into the festival was on foot. Four miles … eight miles … ten miles. Toting sleeping bags, knapsacks, shopping bags, hibachis, soft drinks, a bag of doughnuts, a can of beans, a couple of apples, the endless stream of kids poured into festival area and, always moving closer together, settle on the ground in the amphitheater.

The crew of technicians still was struggling with the massive sound system on the improvised stage. The gates, intended to control admittance, never were put up and the attempt to collect or sell tickets broke down almost at once. By noon, the festival, they announced, was free and open to everyone there. The crowd cheered.

The first scheduled performers, caught in the jam, had to be airlifted in. (It was the helicopters that ensured mobility. Three had been planned for but, eventually 12 were pressed into service.) And still the crowd poured in. No one knows what the total festival population was. The best informed guess was about 400,000. And no one has even tried to guess how many thousands more were turned back on the crowded roads far beyond walking distance.

Overnight, a whole city, the third largest in New York State, had come into being. In a fantastic city in which everything was improvised, drugs were omnipresent and anyone over 30 was out of place, almost as many came together there voluntarily as there were men involuntarily fighting the war in Vietnam. And while they sat through that first night, listening to the performers, rain poured down and the countryside was churned into a sea of red mud.

The first news of the festival to reach the public called it a catastrophe. The listening country was told that a state of emergency had been declared in Bethel, where 300,000 (later a half million) young enthusiasts were in dire straits as a result of rain, lack of food, shelter and sanitation, rising disorder and the uncontrolled use of dangerous drugs.

I didn't get to go to Woodstock but my friends returned three days later, a little tired and somewhat changed. What might have been a disaster had turned instead into a kind of miracle. Listening to my friends, who had been there, I could hear wonder in their voices, and see it in their eyes, as they said, "We were all there together. It was beautiful."

No one denied the struggle merely to survive. That almost everyone did survive was part of the delight. Those who had been at Bethel talked freely about the lack of food and water. The mud. The breakdown of sanitation. The smell of garbage. The cuts and lacerations as thousands walked barefoot on the littered ground. My friends also told me about how people in the crowds (they kept saying things like, "Remember the guy next to you is your brother" and we did!") When I asked my friends what it all meant to them, the answer was almost always, "We were there."

The local people who sent in truckloads of food, the doctors who came into look after the injured and the sick, the police who concentrated on keeping the roads open, the photographers who brought back their "way-out" pictures told stories that convinced me that something very good happened at Woodstock. In spite of everything, the young people achieved that for which they had gone there for, three days of peace and music.

Most people, of course, marveled at the absence of fighting, the almost total absence of any kind of violence in a situation in which, it would seem, the smallest incident might have touched off a riot. But putting it like this, negatively, somehow misses the point.

This generation that was gathered at Woodstock could be fierce and angry on behalf of others. They had marched in sympathy with the children in the ghettos, in protest against the war and the killing in Vietnam, to rouse others to the plight of children. And when they were led to expect violence, they react violently. Excluded from planning that which involves their lives, feared, scorned, and provoked, the young strike back and shout words that, in turn, provoke and horrify.

On this occasion the extraordinary thing was their spontaneous gentleness. They had come of their own free will, because everyone who cared would be there, and it was a way of showing one belonged. Strangers for the most part, they spoke the language of people who trust one another.

The sheer size of the crowd astonished everyone. But after all, such huge gatherings are not unknown. The best parallels are the great religious pilgrimages. There is one very striking difference, however. In the case of religious pilgrimages, tradition sets the style of behavior in every detail.

Hostels exist to receive the pilgrims and strict rules are enforced to protect their safety.

In contrast, at the Woodstock festival everyone was on his own and each crisis called for some new improvisation. Looked at superficially, the who thing had the appearance of something created overnight. The emphasis on spontaneity, the lack of overt forms of organization and the unexpected news of what happened blind us to the fact that there was a king of structure, an image of what it was to be together. Because of that, people not only survived but the occasion had deep meaning for them.

True, the facilities originally provided turned out to be totally inadequate, but crises were met. Extra helicopters were found. Doctors and medical supplies were flown in. The roads were kept open. No one felt trapped. Members of the Hog Farm commune and others like them, only a little older and more experienced than most members of the audience, fed the hungry, counseled the distressed and helped care for the sick and those whose experiments with drugs had miscarried.

Above all, there were the voices, sometimes identified and sometimes anonymous, that rang out between performances, telling the lost where to find their friends and keeping everyone in communication. This, it seems to me, provides a key to understanding why it was that most of the people who experienced Woodstock could say, "It was beautiful." The planning, the improvisation, the stream of communication about what was happening were all part of the event itself. Those who were responsible for these things spoke the language of those who attended the festival.It was at Woodstock, that these "Aquarians" who thought themselves as the first generation in a new age of peace realized, they had a voice, and part of a community of people who trusted each other.It must be admitted that Woodstock might have been a disaster but for two things: one an accident and the other owing to the exercise of intelligence. The accident was the rain. The attendees, in addition to being numerous, gentle and in search of music and peace, were drenched, chilled, exhausted, but still enthusiastic; they moved the hearts of everyone. Moreover, the rain kept away many of the television camera and the majority of those who were merely curious until the festival was all over. The weather was the kind of happy accident one cannot count on happening twice.

The second circumstance was that the responsibility for the festival was in the hands of people who were able to think, respond, and plan in the style of the audience. The very acuteness of the crisis also meant that they remained in responsible control. Their choice of a location, away from any large, settled community, turned out to be the only feasible one. Their choice of musicians drew the crowd. The choice of the Hog Farmers and others like them to act as intermediaries made sense to everyone. Their protective use of human resources probably saved the situation.

Friday, August 15, 1969, was a hot, clear summer day, that changed the lives of many of my friends. I wish I could have gone.

Grammy's Notes:

Woodstock made history despite the rain and sodden conditions, one million people spent that weekend together. Nobody died, there were no arrests, and no fights. I think at least one baby was born. It was a new kind of thinking as well as a new kind of MUSIC that represented the feelings of many young people at that time … Let's not ever forget all the good that came out of the turbulent "60's". The civil rights movement first and foremost, the voting rights act, the environmental movement, the attention finally paid to differently abled people, the clean air act, the clean water act, title ix and a zillion other important changes. People of my generation should not have called Vietnam vets terrible names. They were doing their job. I could go on. I am proud to be part of the solution rather than someone pouring more fuel on the problem. I pray that we will continue to have hope after his next four years term. Anything less will entail to honor the vision and hard work the Woodstock generation has put into these United States.

The Kier Family

Get the Family Hiking Together

FOR THE CHILDREN

PARENTHOOD

To both the father and the mother, I ask the following question: what kind of a future do you want to see for America? What sort of life do you hope to have developed in the days to come. Are we all not in accord with that dream of America which is strong, prosperous and happy- an America at peace with the world in a world at peace. Are not all of us who are parents yarning for a future in which our children may live lives that are courageous, ethical, creative and pacific. Surely most of us want that kind of future for our children and for our beloved country. On this point, if on no other our choice is quite anonymous. Well then, since this is so, let me ask you where is this future to be found. How are you going to make sure a future real? How will you take the dream out of the skies of aspiration to make it come true on his earth? There is, it seems to me, on certain way to do his. It is to realize the simple truth that the future is our children -right now, in the very present. The future is not tomorrow about which we are ignorant, it is not a date far ahead on the calendar. The future is with us, we see it in our children; we are modeling it and forming it everyday as we influence their lives. That is why we parents show a terrible lack of foresight when we fail to give our children all those opportunities for mental and character growth which are so essential for the realization of our dream. First of all, we need parents to give more of themselves to their children. See we delegate to many responsibilities to others. Because one of the messy government setups in Washington in 2017. We must open our eyes to be the strong network that the family can be and must be. We leave things entirely to someone else to provide the child with knowledge, with entertainment, to stimulate our children, to give them goals and ambitions. All these other agencies for education and guidance and inspiration are most important and fundamental. So the trouble, however, lies in the fact that too many parents feel that their job is over when they place the child in a position of exposure to these influences. Now we do not underestimate the importance of the teacher and the school. Nevertheless the school is but one of the great social agencies which help to mold the future by influencing the child. Really we parents our children with us much more of the time than does the school. Yes but I do agree with Hillary Clinton that she has said that it takes a village now a days to raise a child. Parents should never do this job alone. So we need help from all of these agencies. The qualified psychologists tell us, that the first six years of the child's life, are the most important in the life of the individual. Than it should be almost painfully clear that parents and parents above all must assume the responsibility for the kind of people over children become. What a tragedy that we allow ourselves to become so involved with social and financial obligations that we don't find the time to be teachers to our children. We can't let only the teachers in school educate them of only let them learn from other children, this will never work. But our children in the beginning at least, look to us as though we were divine beings, they wait for us to guide them, even though they do not speak of it. And to often they wait in vain. Sometimes I think that the modern child is the loneliest child ever to live. True he has the internet, movies, and television and the most amazing toys. True he can belong to fine youth organizations and go to wonderful schools and take part in exciting sports. But the child who doesn't have the kind of parents who love him enough to teach him and inspire him is a child who is an orphaned and emotionally starved; he is child that is a victim of the modern parental crime of letting others do what should be a paramount responsibility of the father and mother. This is why I call him the loneliest child in the generations of mankind. And this loneliest also explains to a significant degree the alarming extent of juvenile maladjustment and delinquency today. At the White House conference on children and youth, it was pointed out that it takes four years of college, four years of medical school plus a years or two of internship, and then three or more years of specialized training to become a child psychiatrist who may or may not be able to help the child with his problem. But it take only the love, patience and understanding of parents to prevent the development of the problem. Furthermore, I would like to plead for parenthood which takes the time to study the potentialities of the children. There are altogether too many boys and girls who graduate from high school and from college not knowing what they want to do. Our youth is in a desperate plight. Not only are they ignorant of what they desire to do, but also of what they are able to do. Yes, there are vocational counselors and guidance. Counselors and there are aptitude tests to be taken. Yet very few ever avail themselves of these facilities while the majority coast along from year to year with only a vague idea of what to do and with very little stimulus to do anything. We may blame parents for a great deal of this indecision and confusion. Parents ought to make every effort to study the aptitudes of their children, to guide and direct these inclination, to bring out latent abilities and to inspire them with the vision of living that kind of life which derives its happiness from contributing to the happiness of others. Parenthood is the greatest responsibility man has ever been given, because the child is the future. Every cradle shines with the light of the coming dawn, every infant is part of the promise of tomorrows better world. In this very hour when delegates of the United Nations are meeting to solve the problems of the world, these leaders do not exercise greater power than do the humblest mother and father who, sensing their responsibilities to their children are patiently and carefully and consistently shaping the form of the future as they shape the character and lifework of their young. There is another responsibility which parents have towards their children and that is the responsibility of teaching the children through precept and example, the dignity and beauty of family life, of marriage and the sanctity of morality. No one can view our present state of morals without being alarmed. The divorce rate is high and getting higher. Family life is weakened by the impact of our modern pleasure mad world. Some of the problems of the election of 2016 has shown a great deal indecision on voters on who President Trump really is or cares about the people, and has shown as a bad role model that the highest office ever had. His moral beliefs his disrespect for some races has come up many times for the last year and a half. The fact that he has bullied people for years has alarmed me and hard to explain to my grandchildren. Children are much too sophisticated for their years. There is so much that our young people see and hear all around them which breaks down their regard and reverence for moral life. President Trump talking about grabbing woman's body parts. This is no way to act and to hear President Trump is a bad role model anyway you look at what he laughs about. Because we want the future to be blessed with a family life based on fidelity and trust and love. If we want a future in which marriage is held sacred, and the moral integrity of society is healthy and strong. Then it is up to he parents to talk about how bad of a person and the President of the United States not to talk or act as he does. It is up to the parents right now to influence their children who will be the future. Through proper guidance and example. The same holds true for morality and intellectual and cultural interests indeed for all those virtues which make life worth living. Perhaps never before, we need happy wholesome home life for our children, simply because the temptations and forces which undermine morality. My last point I would like to make is so important to save the family. Was that parents ought to have and should cultivate, a sense of humor in dealing with their children.

I am sure that those of you who are parents will agree that we could all do much better in our homes, if we used a sense of humor not only while rearing our children but also in solving our own problems. I am convinced that it would benefit all of us, in these turbulent times, we are to laugh a little bit more instead of becoming so enraged when we read about world problems, and when we gel into a political discussion. This is why so many enjoy the tv show "Saturday Night Live" to be sure we must be earnest and we must think our problems through. Each of us should be reading and thinking and discussing the issues of our times, and searching for as much of the truth as we can obtain. But it need not be without a saving sense of humor. During the most recent presidential campaigns most things were so up setting but for "Saturday Night Live" we could have gone crazy and the outcome for a lot of us are just starting to find humor again. We just had a hard time dealing with this presidential election. Still on facebook the passion for this election temperature are still going up, people dropping friends people blocking people from posting- voices in public places getting tense, violent intolerance on the part of speaker for anybody's point of view except his own. So angry we are, than we lose control. When our tempers are a voused, we say things which we regret in a calmer mood. It would be far better if all of us could hold on to a sense of humor. So if we look at life, in every home, there are problems. Being human, we differ with one another no matter how much we love each other. A family happiness does not mean the absence of disagreements, this bound to arise. To solve problems amicably, sensibly and co-operatively. You have to learn to respect one another's differences. One of the most effective ways to develop this respect is to have a sense of humor. The sense of humor which I recommend is very remote from laughter we enjoy when listen to comedians. It is related to this of course, but very distantly. This humor that we need so much for to day as actually rooted in the sense of compassion and pity, of empathy, of sympathy and profound awareness of tragedy in life. It is also based upon a sense of humility. Have you ever watched a little child first learning how to walk? See him, how he first take hold of the sofa, pulls himself up, and stands there at last, swaying a bit, very uncertain. Then he looks up at you, with your arms outstretched to him as you wait to see him take his first two or three steps all on his own. With all the faith, and the love and the courage in the world, the little child takes a step forward, and can almost take a second when he collapses and falls down. But only for a moment for he tries again and again.

And when at last he falls triumphantly into your arms, both of you laugh! And it is the laughter of pride and love. It is the laughter of perfect happiness. Now on the other hand it is possible to watch the struggles of a child learning how to walk, and just stand there and roar with laughter at the way he staggers and sways and falls. You can watch and laugh at him. If you do this, you are, in essence, regarding him as an object of ridicule, and what he is doing is amusing you, as you look down upon him from your adult position of superiority. You can stand there, upon your feet, but he groping and uncertain and inadequate, falls down again and again. There is a world of difference between laughing at the child and laughing with him as he masters the art of walking surely, there is no semblance what so ever between the laughter of ridicule and the laughter of sympathy and love. And what we need so much today is laughter based upon sympathy and love. If you don't have a good sense of humor and would like to begin to develop it, than the most important place to begin is to learn to laugh at yourself. Oh it is nothing at all to laugh at others- but laughing at yourself. One big reason it is hard is because we think we like to think as ourself as being perfect - as being unable to make a mistake. But relax no one is perfect. The thing that upsets a lot of people about President Trump is as soon as sometime is marked not perfect he is on the internet pushing the blame somewhere else, on some other people. I find him a domineering husband, a humorless father, demanding of his wives, isolating his children and in business and now in government, we encounter him as being hard hearted and cruel. He has sense humor, except but is part of a harsh variety of people which rejoice in another person's downfall. He certainly is unable to laugh at himself and because of this he brings sorrow and misery now into our world. Now the last things I would like to tell you about is the fact that medical profession advise us that laughter is good for our health. The body relaxes when we laugh, and if tightens up when we are angry. I wonder if it has occurred to you as it has to me that the sound of "laugh" and "love" are very close to one another. Love and laugh go together. It has been said "Very few people get into serious trouble when they are laughing. Anger and hate poison the system of the human being. They lead to a variety of fatal ailments. Laughter breaks the ice of aloofness in social gathering laugher breaks down the walls that separate people. When you can laugh together you can work together. Laughter heals the body and soul. We don't begin to live until we developed a sense of humor which clears away the stormy clouds and lets the sunlight in. We Americans, in these hectic days of domestic and international political controversy, are having our sense of humor severely tested. Now is the time, if ever, when we ought to deal with one another with quality of mercy and brotherhood. Of tolerances and sympathy, which will enable us to go forward after domestic elections and United Nations decisions without having caused those wounds which time can not heal. We must see ourselves, not as members of conflicting parties, but as citizens of "One Nation, indivisible, with liberty and justices for all." and as part of humanity. The moment we forget the larger picture, the moment we stop realizing, that there is a tomorrow to be lived, a future to be realized in which this world will go on, our country will go on, we become bored and mentally congested. Granted, that it is important for us to get all the facts we can, and take our sides and strive earnestly for the election of those whom we regard to be best suited to assume the responsibilities of government position. Granted that there is nothing more important for us than to choose sides and to vote and to think seriously about everything pertaining to what goes on in Washington, in our state and local legislatures, in the United Nations and in our foreign policy, nevertheless, no amount of earnestness and seriousness in this area of meeting adequately our citizen's responsibilities should make us lose our sense of humor. To achieve this delicate and fine balance of devotion to one's own point of view. And the higher devotion to the unity which is America, as well as our duties to humanity, requires a sense of humor. This means that we will always remember that the other party is not all wrong and we are not all right and that this country will not go to the dogs if one major party comes into office and the other major party is defeated. A sense of humor will remind that the American people are not going to deliberately surrender our freedom because we at large yearns to be free. I submit that for you and for me in this crucial time - there is nothing better for us to do as we go about this task of keeping America "The land of the Free and the Home of the brave". Because we than can believe with all our heart and soul, that happiness will be our destiny. We should never forget that we are privileged to live in a glorious country. The leader of the free world guided by the law of brotherhood and a sense of humor.

Dads be the father of the year - take your son fishing start young

THE FATHER

Moving on from Motherhood, let us turn our attention to the man who is the head of the household. Let us look at the following question concerning Fatherhood to what extent is the modern father doing the job as the head of his household? By this I mean, how close is he to his children, how much time does he give them, what kind of example is he? I for one feel that the modern father is perhaps in the most unenviable position of an father in history. He loves his children. He enjoys family union. He likes to be a friend, a guide and a comrade.

The modern father would be most pleased to spend a great deal of time with his children and really develop that kind of relationship, which makes for the finest and happiest family life. But, alas, as much as he wants this, he is not in the position to do so because his work keeps him away from home. His children have some of their most important experiences because he is absent from early morning until the dinner hour. Moreover, his work is usually such as to bring him home mentally fatigued and wanting peace relaxation, rather than to assume the challenge of being an interesting companion to his offspring, nor to deal with the whims of his children, he is in no mood. He is tired, hungry and often worried. He is way out of place in the exciting life of his children. After dinner he is more relaxed. But he can not attract his children because they are now at the internet playing video games or at the TV set and now cool to the father's attention. I sure there are a number of exceptions to what I have just stated. There are some fathers because of the nature of the work they do

Or because they are the kind of man that they are, who do have ample time for their children. This I believe to be the exception and not the rule. In the majority of cases, children seldom have much contact with their father so that the larger part of the responsibility of raising the children must be met by the mother. If I have been fair in my portrayal of this particular aspect of family life and I hope I have, then I believe it would be in order to ask ourselves what the modern father

Can do to desire from his family life as well as to contribute to it, at least some of the good, the joy, and the blessing that if should contain. I observed at the start that I feel sorry for the modern father. He has to work all day under pressure. He works hard that he usually dies many years before his wife, and thus there is a tragic aspect to his existence. According to actuarial statistics, men die, on average, from five to seven years before their wives. He has to meet the rigors of tough competition, has to work hard to get to the top

Has to work hard in any case if only to support his family (even if his wife has a second job to help out) He does not gel enough of the abiding happiness of life. Working these days, at most jobs is not much fun because of its hectic tempo. The average man has little opportunity to interest himself in the things of the spirit because he is so busy providing enough fuel to keep the home fires burning, while the life of the mother is also full of hardships as I have stated. She derives many satisfactions from her experiences.

This appraisal, I know, goes contrary to the popular idea that this is a man's world. From what I see it only appears to be a man's world. Actually men work their lives away trying to give a portion of this world to their mothers, wives and children. They come home mentally if not physically, exhausted. If I have drawn a picture of the modern father which makes him a rather weary and troubled kind of human being. I may be guilty of exaggerating the picture a little, but I don't think is it too far from the mark. The father lacks time, so the father must make the time every to get his family away from the interred to TV, with all of those games.

Go camping, what a better place than our natural parks. We cannot be certain of survival if we turn our backs on family life. The ancient country of Greece, in all of its glory, in all of it's magnificence of art and culture, went down in defeat to large measure because of divorce, sexual immorality and contempt for family life had broken the strength of that great nation. The same tragic pattern was carried out in Rome when with moral degeneracy and contempt the grandeur of Rome was destroyed.

Our beloved country need not fear for its future, even with a weak president, if we the people, restore family life, to that healthy condition which has always been the backbone of our democracy. You don't have to vacation in Disney World. Standing in line to take a fake ride on a raft. Go to a campground with a real river running through it and do it as a family. What a bond this would bring into the family life. You as a father should make this happen.

We should all resolve to take advantage of every opportunity to be together as a family get away of all distractions of everyday life. For in the peace and strength of family life our nation shall have peace and strength and in this our world can come nearer to the attainment of the universal peace. After the election of 2016 we need this more than ever. Maybe there is hope of showing President Trump how to be a better person too.

MOTHERHOOD

Each year, Americans celebrate Mother's Day. We know that throughout the United States millions of dollars are spent to purchase gifts and flowers and candy by children of all ages in honor of their mothers. People object to the commercial features of Mother's Day. However justified, such criticisms overlook the fact that these mercantile aspects help considerably in American life. There is something thrilling about a whole nation alerted to the thought of motherhood and its sanctity. It is always a good thing to take time to fake time to show appreciation and love, one's gratitude for favors.

How much more is it good for use to pause and pay homage to our mothers. Of course there is the danger of being to gushy and sweet on mother's day. It is not easy to resist the temptation to exaggerate beyond any semblance of reality how affectionate we feel toward her who brought us into this world and raised us. On the other hand, we can be so zealous for restraint that we do not manifest enough of our sentiments as we concern ourselves with the many challenges of motherhood today.

I want to make it clear that I am fully cognizant of the enormity of the thousand and on tasks which the modern mother is called upon to do in 2017. When I think of what a mother is expected to be in order to do her job successfully, resourcefulness and her capacity. Compared with what the fathers do and are expected to do, the work of motherhood is infinitely more complex and demanding. A Father leaves his home in the morning and he goes to work which is usually confined to some speciality. Whether a man be in a business or a profession.

He does that job and nothing else, he is able to concentrate on his special task without any interference, the mother, however, has an endless variety of responsibilities to meet. In the great choral of life, the father sings a solo, where as the mother must be able to sing many parts of the music. To be a successful mother today, a woman is supposed to be a loving wife, to her husband and a devoted mother to her children. She must be a psychologist, an economist, a decorator, civic worker, and educator. She must know how to cook, wash, iron, clean house, repair, nurse and comfort. She must be a counselor, adviser, peace maker, and informed. A devotee of the arts, a charming conversationalist well dressed and attractive woman. All of this and more at on and the same time. In a single day, a mother must meet kind of emergency, ranging from domestic crises to problems of church and state. That she is able to do all of these, or some of these as well as she does, and that she sometimes fails to do some of these things successfully, and that still keeps her sense of humor and sanity, is all very impressive.

Since the election of 2016 putting Trump I the highest seat in our country. Mother's everywhere our coming together to march on how strong they will be one day after trump took over power women marched across the USA millions came together. Yes women and mothers have power. It is new with the 45 president as a weak role model as never before the family must become stronger. A long time ago there was a very delightful play presented in New York called "life of Mother"

With a period of two hours. This drama deals with the amazing complexity and variety of a mother's responsibility as she helps her husband and four sons to meet their problems, while at the same time she solves her own. The mother in the play, like some mothers in real life, affects the mannerisms of a scatterbrained, naive person who apparently doesn't know what things are all about. Nevertheless, in her own way, she manages to accomplish exactly what she wants. Nothing more and nothing less. There is a method to mother's madness, which all good in good time come to recognize and to honor. You come away from that play realizing that you should never underestimate a mother, especially if that mother has a definite objective in view. It must have been a mother who thought up the old proverb "there are more ways than one to skin a cat" Once a mother makes up her mind about something she wants, or doesn't want, for her husband, herself her children, or her home, nothing this dies of God's Heaven can stop her. A mother is a power and never fool yourself that she isn't'.

Next to god she is the greatest power on earth. Now, it is precisely because a mother can exercise such a potent influence in the home that we ask her to exercise her power in behalf of saving civilization. Those women who marched across the USA and mainly in Washington, D.C. were making a statement, and showing the 45th President that they have power. Unless men learn from women how to be more loving and cooperative, they will go on making the kind of mistake and mess of the world which they have so effectively achieved thus far.

And this is of course, where women can realize their power for good in the world, and make their greatest gains. It is the function of women to teach men how to be human. Women must not permit themselves to be deviated from this function by those who tell them that their place is in the home in subservient relations to man. It is, indeed, in the home that the foundations of the kind of world in which we live are laid, and in this sense it will always remain true that the hand that rocks the cradle is the hand that rules the world.

And it is in this sense that women must assume the job of making men, who will make the world fit for human beings to live in. The greatest single step forward in this direction will be made when women consciously assume this task. The task of teaching their children to be like themselves, loving and cooperative. We can agree wholeheartedly. The one thing the child must have in order to live is oxygen, and next in importance to oxygen is mother love. The mother-child relationship. My belief is that the essence of the greatness of mother lover is her willingness to give sacrificially to the welfare of her children.

Yes the women who places her children's welfare first. Now the first six years in a person's life are the most important. The experiences of childhood, we are told by every authority, influence are character and personality development. Most failures in life are due, then not so much to deficiencies in intelligence and capacities as they are to our personality problem who source is found in the first six years of life. The mother of today must put up with the internet-tv-movies and everything extra to hold the attention and keep her family on track. This is a big job.

Take time every year to get the family away, a vacation to get the family back to nature. Camping, hiking, boating, cooking, together over a campfire, having time to talk about making life worth living. I remember around a campfire with a group of teenagers, my children there too. Trying to answer the questions. This is what we came up with: it was worth living. The happy life, the useful life is not a gift. You are not going to win it as a prize, nor buy it like some piece of furniture. Everyone around this campfire came up with; you yourself, will have to make your life your life worth living. You will have to earn it. Struggle for it. Plan for it worthy and enjoyable life is the life which you make worthwhile. Yes we had to get away from the stress of daily life, to take a good look at life. Make time to take time for a vacation from everyday life.

SAVE THE WHALE

Today we arrived at Pacific City Oregon on a cool morning. Our RV camp was about three blocks from the beach. With the beach on our minds we ate breakfast in the RV in a hurry. The next part of my story is something Jimmy and I never thought we would see in our lifetime.

As we came within a block from the beach we could see a large crowd of people moving to the beach. Along this block were a few trucks with Greenpeace marked on the doors of the truck. A truck hauling a boat. An investigation was going on. My grandmother, being an environmental activist, knew some people controlling the crowd. So she went over to talk to some of her friends from Greenpeace. They explained to her that on the beach today a whale had beached himself. My grandmother's friends that were in charge, took us down to the whale at the ocean edge. Viewing life from a thousand feet away we were pulled into this drama. Now my grandmother could hear the four whales out in the ocean. Whale sounds that they make when they are in distress. The whales have a languages all their own. The next thing I know our grandmother is rushing us back to the RV. Here my grandmother remembered the "Little People" talking about saving a whale that was caught in a fish net. The "Little People" knew whale sounds- the whale language. The "Little People" could communicate with this beached whale.

We than hurried to see how we could help save this beached whale. So we put the "Little People" into their carrying case and headed back to the beach. There we met with the Greenpeace people. They were not shocked by the 4 inch tall "Little People". Greenpeace had heard of the "Little People". Everyone agreed that the "Little People" should talk to the beached whale to see what his problem was and then Greenpeace would take the "Little People" in a boat out to the whales in the ocean and speak with them. The whales crying in the ocean were trying to get the beached whale back in the ocean. My grandmother spoke to use. "Look kids, we have to get that whale back in the ocean before it gets dark." Grandmother then in a sad voice said "the uncertainty that darkness brings can humble even the hardest soul."

Now the story the beached whale tells the "Little People", he is depressed, he lost his wife and son. He cannot live without them. His sadness became so intense he beached himself. Everyone was working hard to help this whale. The Greenpeace people were hosing him down with water from the ocean. The "Little People" hopped into the greenpeace boat and were taken out to see the four whales in the ocean. The story that the "Little People" got from these whales yelling out in the ocean. They had good story for the beached whale. His wife and his son are not dead. They are up north looking for him. It was wonderful the "Little People" know whale language. They hurried back to shore. The Greenpeace people were there with ropes and two more boats to drag the beached whale back into the ocean.

See we learned from grandmother that depression is a bad thing if the animal or person does not have some kind of help from others. It made us talk that night about what we must do to help someone that needs help. Here are some of the things my grandmother told us:

1. Reach out and stay connected to supportive people.
2. Move vigorously during the day, don't sit for more than an hour.
3. Do things that make you feel good, even if you don't feel like it
4. Learn about the mood boosting benefits of omega 3 fats
5. Challenge negative thinking
6. Spend time outdoors in the sunlight.

Yes my grandmother was a nurse and she knows how to help people and animals. The whale was given hope, everyone helped to get the whale back in the ocean. His friends were waiting for him to help him meet up with this wife and son. The drama today was unbelievable. Thank goodness the "Little People" were there and knew whale language. After all the "Little People" feel that their purpose in life was to help people and animals in this world because some problems need help from others. It was high drama but it was fun today to have the day end with good things happening.

The wisdom that can be taken from the poem "Stopping by Woods on A Snowy Evening" by Robert Frost is simple and comes into view right away. Every professional, every executive and every literate layman should place this poem in everyday view. Robert Frost might have known a very busy doctor or "Type A" personality. By this I mean the person who has a well defined pattern of his lifestyle marked by a compelling sense of time urgency; "hurry sickness", aggressiveness, and competitiveness.

Cardiologists Friedman and Rosenman explain their startling finding- that the primary cause of heart disease is a distinct behavior pattern, a particular complex of personality, lifestyle, and attitude, which they call Type A behavior.

Take that break with your family. Go on vacation, see the National Parks, spend time with your family to come closer together. Give your body a change that it so much needed. Slow your life down, get away from the phone, TV and the many demands of life, to give the body a break will stop it from breaking.

And to get energy and rise in the sunrise. To sit around a campfire and just talk, and get to know each other again as real people in this beautiful, beautiful United States. Listen closely now: It's better to look back on your life and say- "I can't believe I was able to do that!" Than to look back and say- "I wish I did that."

Grammy Notes:

Parent – the family is in your hand. You must save the family. Our future parents you must cultivate a deeper reverence for life and teach the fact that we must appreciate all of your days on this planet. Because as we have witnessed in life we could be called away at any moment. Teach your children to keep their houses in order, mental, physical, spiritual and emotional. Sharpen their mind with new ideas and perspective, bless their body with nutrition and exercise, and teach them to let your soul be right and keep their emotions in check. Too often we vex others with fear and too often we allow others to prevent us from flying towards their destinies and dreams. Instead encourage one another edify other even when they aren't in our presence, I realize that action has reaction, and that acts of love destroy fear. Hate is fear manifest. Teach your kids to listen to their hearts "see" people and acknowledge them. The impact on their life may be profound, and though you may never see the result, their life will be enhanced. Appreciate their differences, learn from them, respect them and ultimately let their differences unite us. Because that is who they are. Forgive, teach them, bless this world proactively and let your life be a healthy thumbprint on the universe.

Grammy's Notes

Before you assume: Learn the facts

Before you judge: understand why

Before you hurt someone: feel

Before you speak: think

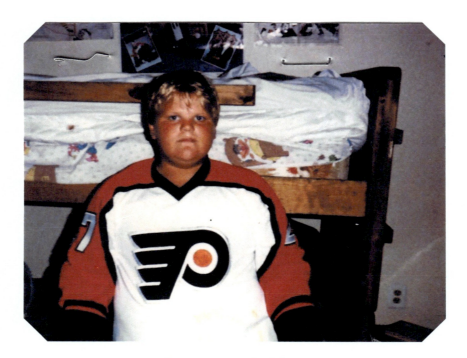

Jimmy a wonderful son

A Grammy Note:

20 things to tell your son and daughter

1. Play a sport. It will teach you how to win. Honorably, lose gracefully, respect authority, work with others, manager you time and stay out of trouble and maybe even throw a catch.

2. You will set the tone for the sexual relationship, so don't take something away from her

3. Use careful aim when you pee. Somebody's got to clean it up, you know! Boys stand up girls sit down.

4. Save money when you're young because you'll need it someday

5. Allow me to introduce you to dishwasher, oven, washing machine, iron, vacuum, mop and broom. Now please use them.

6. Pray and be spiritual leader

7. Don't ever be a bully and don't ever start a fight, but if some idiot clock you, please defend yourself.

8. Your knowledge and education is something that nobody can take away from you

9. Treat women kindly son forever is a long time to live alone and it's even longer to live with someone who hates your guts. Girls be your man's best friend and partner and your knight to save you from the world. Love is better than hate.

10. Take pride in your appearance always

11. Be strong, loving and tender at the same time.

12. Everyone work together. A women can do anything that a man can do. This includes her having a successful career and man can change diapers at 3 am. Mutual respect is the key to a good relationship

13. Yes ma'am yes sir still goes a long way

14. The reason that they're called "private parts" it's because they are "private" don't scratch them in public

15. Peer pressure is a scary thing. Be a good leader and others will follow

16. Bring her flowers for no reason is always a good idea. Women give those backrubs are good for him.

17. It is better to be kind than to be right

18. A sense of humor goes a long way in the healing process

???

Tonight in my journal I want to tell you about our trip that is very real!

1. My family and friends we have met along the many miles.

2. The roads that we have traveled going from the East Coast to the West Coast.

3. The mountains that at times we got out of the RV, walked up to them, reached out and touched them. SO REAL!

4. The trees, so many different kinds, along the way. The Mighty RedWoods-some having tunnels that you can drive through! An amazing giant right before our eyes!

5. The bears and other animals running through the woods. The deer, elk, and buffalo running in the fields. In Yellowstone National Park we met a big buffalo just walking up the road.

6. The trees that we saw when we crossed the Rockies. So Real! We were looking at the tops of them!

7. The wind moving things along-blowing through the trees. In the desert the wind blew very strong at times moving sand everywhere also in the desert we saw Marposal Lily Cactus-cactus flowers, giant cactus that have roots that go twice as deep as the plant showing on top of the ground.

8. The desert animals, Armadillo Lizards, a ground dwelling lizard active in the daytime feeds on insects and spiders. It is very slow moving weighing it around 8-17 pounds. Armadillo armor protects them from birds, mammals and other reptiles. Snakes are everywhere.

9. The sun so real waking us in the morning and then giving us the most beautiful sunsets at the end of the day.

10. But you can never believe or understand how real the world is unless you go out and see it and touch it with your hands. Smell it with your nose. Taste it with your mouth. I hope you get the chance!

11. The sounds of the vastness. The way lights shadows move across the mountain tops and wide expanses. I will never forget.

12. The Grand Canyon historic train tour is something not to miss. This vintage train from Williams to the Grand Canyon lets you see what history has changed the canyon in itself. This railway train made its first journey to the South Rim in 1901 and today you can make the same trip only in person do you know how real this journey is. Nothing on the internet or TV and read in a book can give you a feeling of realness like being there.

Well folks, we came a long journey. 8,000 miles. This is the end of my journal, we are almost home. We have a couple of more hours. We left in the rain and are coming home in the rain, but in between there was nothing but sunshine and a feeling of success. There was a wind behind us that powered us, that brought our family closer together, it gave the little people a chance to show their purpose, and to fulfill their destiny here on earth. Yes, saving the whale is a moment we will all never forget, but it was a moment for the little people too. The wind will not blow us away, but just moves us along making us better people. I would like to think that it is God blowing that wind. He gives us a chance to be the family, that we can be and to see our world through our eyes, and to feel beauty. God Bless America! It blew us along and brought us safely home. It blew us along and gave us hope. This is my hope, that those 8,000 miles will never be wasted, but shared with you. That as a family unit, you will gather up, grab your bikes, even if you just ride through the woods, climb a mountain, climb a hill, go, go look at that ocean, the beautiful ever moving ocean, that river that flows. I just wish for all of you to have the opportunity to be together and to experience the beauty of this country, to relax in the sunset

(back of book)

This story is about a journey of 8,000 miles across the United States. It is a family's adventures traveling to the National Parks in a 37 foot RV, going on tours by trains, bikes, mules, hiking, and white water rafting. It is treating you to the journal that Jenny keeps on the trip. They bring the little people along also. They are just three and four inches tall that Jenny and Jimmy found a few years ago in their barn. The first book was The Little People in the Barn. I wrote and told the story of how the little people got to America, how they traveled the United States and ended up in a barn in Glenmore, Pennsylvania and that is where Jenny and Jimmy found them. This is my second book about the little people. After being a mother, a teacher and a nurse, I decided to become an author. My five children are raised. I have retired from nursing and now have the time to write these stories. It has always been a dream of mine to share the feeling that the little people have to express. Who are the little people? Are they us? The ones that the government are in control of, but when the little people gather together in unconditional love there is no greater story. The little people's village is a mastermind of undisturbed sighting. They rationalize and talk things out, they have great faith in God and they are not supernatural in anyway. They are just like us and this is what I want to convey.

Who are the little people? They might just be you. Can we learn from them? Yes, we can. The journey across the United States was a wonderful family oriented trip. It brought the little people closer together, and it brought us closer together and we learned about how the Indians feel, their struggle, we saw the great skywalk of the Grand Canyon. Yes, I have enjoyed my second book.

Grammy's Notes

Sorry to say this, Trump is a person who is without grace, dignity, humility, insight and personal responsibility. He is not fit representative of any public body.

Sunset

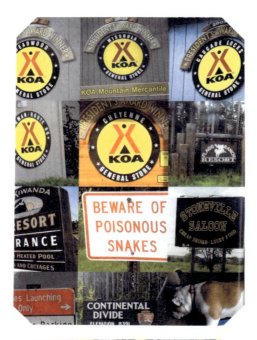